ENYA

ENYA

A TREATISE ON UNGUILTY PLEASURES

CHILLY GONZALES

Invisible Publishing
Halifax & Prince Edward County

Cataloguing data available from Library and Archives Canada

Bibliophonic Series editor: Del Cowie
Cover by Megan Fildes
Typeset in Laurentian & Slate by Megan Fildes
With thanks to type designer Rod McDonald

Printed and bound in Canada

Invisible Publishing
Halifax & Prince Edward County
www.invisiblepublishing.com

Published with the generous assistance of the Canada Council for the
Arts, the Ontario Arts Council, and the Government of Canada.

LULLABY VOICE

I DON'T REMEMBER MY MOTHER EVER SINGING ME A LULLABY. She had many voices, just not one for lullabies. She had a squawking Jewish mother voice for storytelling, an icy almost-British accent for when she was having fights, an exaggerated Miss Piggy yell to get our attention in the basement (this was the voice she was best known for among my friends)... but she didn't have a soothing voice in her repertoire. She was never natural, always performing. So, no lullabies for me.

And anyway, a lullaby isn't a performance. It's basically folk music; it serves a social purpose. The lullaby already existed before the conscious pretense of artistic musical expression. Maybe I'm romanticizing, but folk music (communal storytelling through music) always seemed less selfish as compared to pop music (Lionel Richie dancing upside down). At least, my pop music felt selfish: I started making music to get attention, to live out a fantasy. I made sure that my virtuosity was proof of my talent and the worst insult I could imagine was someone telling me it reminded them of a lullaby. My motivation was so ego-driven, how was my music supposed to bind people together? I always envied musicians who made music for a social purpose: gospel musicians for God, DJs for dancing, folk musicians for community, and lullabies for soothing children.

Contra pop music, a lullaby has no backing band or beat. Usually zero accompaniment. It has to work by itself a cappella. You can't rely on a strange, unexpected harmonic twist to provide drama in the musical storytelling, like the "nothing really matters" chord in the opening of "Bohemian Rhapsody." You can't count on a sonic surprise like the awkward stutter of muted guitar strings before the chorus of Radiohead's "Creep." No saxophone solos, no filter sweep, no auto-tune. A lullaby, in fact, is pure melody, the voice itself.

I've always been old-fashioned when it comes to respecting melody. Melody is the surface of a song, the facade of the building. So, when someone asks you if you've heard a new song, they'll just sing the melody. You know the one that goes "groove is in the hea-ar-ar-ar-art?" For most people, the melody *is* the whole song.

Harmony—the chords that support the melody—is the invisible foundation of the building. These chords have the unglamorous power to maximize emotions in a song, but chords aren't enough to be a song by themselves, and you definitely can't hum a chord. Imagine "With or Without You" if Bono never started singing. Harmony is melody's bitch, with no life of its own.

Hearing a melody a cappella, divorced from its harmony and expelled from its sound-world, is a kind of test. Does it still sound like music, when it's sung, just like that, by a civilian (an amateur)? The ultimate test: How does it sound when sung by your mother?

If it passes this test, the melody indeed becomes the whole song—music's synecdoche. All lullabies have passed this test; they've survived for centuries. They're still there after capitalism, sleeping pills, and the invention of recording, never outgrowing their original purpose.

That's probably why we don't listen to recordings of lullabies. They don't exist as recordings the way pop songs do. A pop song is a specific moment in time captured by a specific artist; it belongs to that artist and we acknowledge their ownership, it will always sound the same. Hearing it live, or hearing a cover version of it, will still always refer us back to the original.

There is only one "Take On Me" and it is by a-ha, and if we hear some eighties tribute band performing it, we are comparing it to the 1981 studio performance of "Take On Me." There is no imagining the song without the precise combination of cheesy drum sounds and the voice of Morten Harket (I just

Googled his name). A pop song is alive only at the moment that it is born—from then on it is frozen like a caveman in ice. It's near-impossible to get people to hear a cover of an iconic pop song with fresh ears, as if for the first time. I know; I've tried.

When I first switched to piano-only concerts in 2004, one of my best/worst ideas was to re-arrange eighties pop songs using jazz and classical gestures. One of the songs I devised was a faux-Baroque arrangement of Enya's "Orinoco Flow" (the "sail away" song). But my cover didn't really have a chance to be heard objectively. It could only remind people of the original version, still living rent-free in everyone's collective nostalgia-mind.

Folk music doesn't have this baggage: there's no original recording of a lullaby. It's not even something we can evaluate on the basis of musical taste. It either *works* at its function or it *fails*. The baby sleeps or it doesn't (as in comedy, the crowd laughs or it doesn't). We don't know or care who composed it. It only matters who is singing it.

So, what kind of voice *works* when it comes to the lullaby? A soothing voice, a reassuring voice, something that takes away pain, doubt, something that makes the listener feel safe, something gentle and patient—a voice you can trust as natural. An unnatural voice may fool some of the people, but authenticity is something that we just know when we hear it.

Some years ago, a friend got so excited to play me something new he had discovered. He couldn't believe I hadn't heard it yet, everyone was talking about it, I was going to love it so much, he said. I hate being told I'll love something before I've had the chance to decide for myself. He pressed play. Guitar music, not my cup of tea. But it had enough harmonic flair, the feel of the drums was a relatively disciplined combination of modern sounds with just enough surprising moments to give it humanity, there were sonic references I recognized and some I even appreciated... and then the singer came in. This singer thought he could fool me by hiding inside this respectable backing track. But his insecurity was audible to me, he was faking it. He had figured out a way to imitate the sound of "letting go" without letting go. An unmusical person's idea of unrestrained artistry. Barf.

An untrustworthy voice does not please the gods of music. "An untrustworthy voice" is a phrase that reminds me too much of my mother. Music is too important a place for me, it can't be tainted by a voice that pretends.

Imagine a lullaby sung by this kind of pretender. There's something traumatizing about the intrusion of fakery into the child's room at such a fragile moment as bedtime. A singer's voice has to be believable, even though singing itself is performative. There's a contradiction here. Of course, we understand that a singer goes to a studio, steps into a vocal booth, sings their part hundreds of times, receives input from producers, chooses the best moments, and massages them into a Frankenstein's monster called a "comp" (compilation? composition?). But if it works, this monster appears to us as a cohesive performance. Sure, we like to imagine it was a single transcendent moment of emotional truth. As with our favourite actors, we demand naturalism despite knowing that we are watching something staged, something that probably took weeks to shoot with dozens of crew members standing around just out of the frame of the camera.

A lullaby doesn't need to be Frankenstein-ed into existence. As a child I didn't realize any of this. I just accepted that my bedtime was lullaby-less. And somewhere buried inside me there was a longing for a soothing voice.

As a young teenager, when the other boys were smoking weed or discovering their sexuality, I sat at the piano binging on late eighties jazz fusion, the more virtuosic and macho the better, trying to decipher the complexities—the worst offenders being Chick Corea Elektric Band (yes, that is how it's spelled, with a K). This kind of musical masturbation kept my brain occupied as my emotions hummed along in the background.

I started getting good at showing off. I could play the iconic drum fill from Phil Collins' "In the Air Tonight." I could play piano for a really popular cool kid from my school as he sang "I Don't Like Mondays" by the Boomtown Rats at a party. I was so musically sensitive I could even modulate the chords of the song if the cool kid accidentally went off-key (I knew how to make him look better than he was). I became that musical genius kid who could play anything. This meant I could corral some friends into starting a band with me. One of these first bands was called Decoy (jazz-rock in the style of Sting but named after a Miles Davis fusion album), and we won a battle of the bands when I was fourteen years old. Winning felt really good. The prize was two days of studio time.

Though I was technically the drummer, I was actually a little musical dictator, micromanaging my poor buddies who just wanted to be in a band for the laughs. We covered "Purple Haze" even though I didn't even like the Jimi Hendrix original, and I butchered the song by adding complicated chords, trying to make it sound like Chick Corea. The professional engineer at the studio could see some talent in me, but also realized my hyperactive controlling personality wasn't doing the music any favours. He gave me the nickname Mr. Bennies. I was too in awe of musicianship to understand the value of the lullaby voice.

A couple of years later, after the gateway drug of Chick Corea and fusion, I found my way to actual jazz. But the jazz I liked was still tending towards the virtuosic. As the emperor tells Mozart in the movie *Amadeus*: "Too many notes." I became obsessed with the muscular, ecstatic, and frankly coked-up albums of John Coltrane. It was less embarrassing than being into jazz fusion because Coltrane was a legitimate icon.

But one of my jazz piano teachers took pity on me and recommended a John Coltrane collaboration album with the crooner Johnny Hartman. It was from the same time period as the wanky stuff, but this was a whole different Coltrane. Here he wasn't the star, he was merely an accompanist to an old-fashioned torch singer. He was commenting on the story, part of a dialogue rather than a stream-of-consciousness monologue. Where was my beloved saxophone stud? This album didn't seem to want to impress me, so I wasn't impressed. What was this underwhelming crap? It was slow, soporific—almost lullaby-like (yawn!).

At the next piano lesson, the teacher shook his head when I reported back. He told me to listen for the space in the Coltrane/Hartman songs. I admired my teacher so much at first, I just pretended to know what he meant. But I kept listening, and slowly I started to hear it. After each saxophone phrase there was space that I could fill with my own emotional reactions. It was the beginning of a long and painful goodbye to my worship of show-offs. Why had I spent so much time venerating these fast-fingered con artists? Looking back, I see them for the fakers and charlatans they were.

I was one of those fakers. I'd been (mis)using music to impress people, instead of connecting with them. Like Prince sang in "When Doves Cry," "maybe I'm just like my mother," she who performed for people instead of being natural with them. I had unknowingly replicated her life strategy in my approach to music, but not for much longer. Thanks to my jazz piano teacher, I was drawn to a new musical space where connection mattered more than technical skill. A space without ego, a space without Mr. Bennies or my mother. And that space came to be filled with lullaby voices—Johnny Hartman, not Chick Corea, Beach House not Björk, Roberta Flack not Aretha Franklin. And most of all, Enya.

I assume anyone reading this has heard Enya's voice, so I won't spend too much time trying to describe it.

I'm not a record reviewer (thank God) but the cliché that springs to mind is the voice of an angel. And I think I know what the voice of an angel would probably sound like: ethereal and pure.

When I say ethereal, I mean the quality of airiness. Any time a voice sings a note, there is a combination of tone (the note itself) and air. This air is like a subtle bed of white noise. It's like a breath-cloud, a feeling of context, of place, a visual fog around the pure voice tone. There can be more or less air: When a singer sings quietly, it's easier to add breath than sing loudly (rapper DMX doesn't really do ethereal).

And when I say pure, I mean the quality of being natural and unforced. Enya rarely uses the crutch of vibrato—quite literally the vibrating of a note to add emotion. Vibrato isn't the enemy, it definitely makes me cry once in a while. Nina Simone's voice is almost permanently vibrating with fragility as it carries her vulnerability. The violin or the flute can't really do their expressive job without it. Vibrato is waves, warmth, depth, life!

But opera singers in the eighteenth and nineteenth centuries ruined it. Their constant, loud vibrato could almost be mistaken for an ambulance siren. There was a good reason for that back then: no microphones and big theatres. They whipped out those vibrating voices to make sure the cheap seats could hear them. But we have had microphones for a century now. My friend Mocky calls Frank Sinatra the first techno artist, because he used the microphone to place his voice right against the ear of the listener, whispering sweet nothings in a kind of proto-ASMR.

Now thankfully big fat vibrato is an anachronism. When I was a kid, I would do this stupid imitation of Pavarotti, replacing the Italian words with made-up nonsense, and it would end with me basically screaming with mucho vibrato with my arms outstretched— a parody of exaggerated emotion.

Vibrato is a bit like my formerly beloved jazz fusion: technically very difficult to learn but even more difficult to listen to. But to sing with no vibrato at all, to let the music itself do the emotional work is the purist's choice. Think of French chanteuse Françoise Hardy at her best, Astrud Gilberto, my good friend Leslie Feist—voices of angels with no need to exaggerate. Enya would never do that. I know that when I listen to Enya, I imagine myself a baby, being lulled to sleep by an Irish fairy princess. She is ethereal, pure but more than that, she is our good mother, and she wants us to know that everything will be okay.

UNGUILTY PLEASURE

TASTE STARTS OUT AS AN INVOLUNTARY REACTION. Like laughter. A joke is funny if you laugh and fails if you don't. You like the taste of bananas or you don't and I, for one, hate bananas.

Musical taste starts out the same way. A child's taste isn't a conscious choice. As a kid, I remember seeing Billy Joel on TV for the first time and I thought he looked sad and tired, but he sang and played the piano with so much energy. The hair on the back of my neck stood at attention. It felt like he was singing right to me, and he played the piano (my classmates all believed that electric guitar was cooler). Without even being aware of it, I had found something very much to my taste. And look what happened when I grew up: I devoted myself to the piano, a sad and tired look, high energy.

When I first became friends with Peaches, she told me how as a kid she was obsessed with the Andrew Lloyd Webber musical *Jesus Christ Superstar*. In 2009, she performed a one-woman version of that musical with me at the piano entitled *Peaches Christ Super-*

star. She was re-enacting her own version of my Billy
Joel moment. When I first saw Jarvis Cocker perform,
I felt as if I was watching an awkward twelve-year-old
boy dance in front of the mirror using a hairbrush
as a fake microphone. A nerd's revenge fantasy
come true! Every musician I know is still channel-
ling epiphanies from this musical Garden of Eden
of their childhood, before they bit into the apple of
self-awareness.

I remember when I became painfully self-aware.
The world opened up in terrifying ways, forcing me
into questions of self-definition. Who was I, inside?
And how much of that could I show to the outside
world? Would I get what I want by being me? Or
should I change myself to be liked? Do my clothes
fit to the image I want to project? Will everyone see
through me? Is it okay to like jazz fusion and Billy
Joel? Wouldn't I rather be someone who listens to
cool shit, like industrial music, or maybe Pavement?

What is cool shit anyway? Have you ever noticed
how the year-end best albums lists seem to be ninety
percent identical? Is it actually possible for all critics
to happen to like the same ten records? Shouldn't
these lists be titled Consensus Choices for Coolest
Albums? But I wanted to be cool, and here was the
blueprint I needed. I would read these lists, internal-
ize them. It was like gravity. These albums were obviously worth liking so I would learn to like them.

As a teenager it only took me a few conversations to understand that my real taste wasn't cool. I told myself I needed educating in cool shit. But in reality, I was trying on a mask to see how it fit. My taste devolved from an involuntary physical reaction to a wilful but desperate act of self-definition. I allowed myself to lose the musical innocence of goosebumps. These acquired tastes were my ticket to join a club. I was conforming, but I felt safe. I re-imagined who I wanted to be. I started to retrofit my musical taste, stuffed myself with cool music, went into hibernation and re-emerged... as a guy who listens to Pavement. Fuck that jazz, fuck that soft rock, fuck the Bee Gees.

Now I fooled myself into seeing just how uncool I had been the whole time. Jazz and soft rock were musical genres associated with expertise, training, elitism, nostalgia—backward-looking, conservative, rule-following music. Music about music, only concerned with technical prowess. No feeling, no attitude, and definitely zero rebelliousness. Was I such a goody two-shoes? Was I really Mr. Bennies? These uncool genres were my pathetic reality. And I did not enjoy that reality one bit (not until later, when I found the balls to let out my inner Bee Gee).

I regret those years in disguise as an alternative rock fanboy. I feel pity for that insecure gangly kid. I wish I could've owned my goosebumps, to not censor them. The pleasure I'd felt so freely listening to jazz wankers was suddenly burdened by shame and guilt. I had fallen victim to the guilty pleasure. The music journalist's favourite go-to question: Confess your guilty pleasure. The accusation is clear. Have you been hiding some secret from us? It's like they can smell my soft spot for The Carpenters. "Tell us who you *really* are..."

Well, if you type "guilty pleasure" into Google the top result is a Spotify playlist of mercilessly effective commercial pop songs, Paris Hilton, Backstreet Boys, Black Eyed Peas. So that's what constitutes a guilty pleasure: openly, unashamedly capitalist pop music with no apology. Songs that are *trying* to be loved, maybe even to the point of desperation.

The guilty pleasure begs for approval—no wonder we feel guilty! To say, "I shouldn't like Enya," is to say we look down at her ubiquity and commercial dominance. None of us would openly admit to falling for lowest-common-denominator vulgarity. If everyone likes something, the natural instinct is to find something rarer, like the Welsh singer Arabella (no one knows her yet, she's so obscure I just invented her name).

Or else we come upon the cliché of "I liked their early stuff." A rapper friend of mine loved the Black Eyed Peas when they burst onto the scene in the late nineties as a backpack rap collective. Then Fergie joined the band, they became everyone's favourite pop act, and he had to abandon ship. He didn't feel like a connoisseur anymore, just a punter. Enya's early stuff was already for *everyone*. She wasn't ever the unlikely underdog. The world fell in love with her instantly in 1988 with "Orinoco Flow" when she emerged fully formed in the mainstream.

Is she cool or uncool? Her music is New Age, for fuck's sake. Uncool. I remember hearing the words New Age for the first time in relation to Enya. Clearly this was the invention of some marketing douchebag. This was around the time that yoga, sushi, and meditation emerged into public consciousness. This movement needed a soundtrack and Enya was in the wrong place at the wrong time. New Age music had that spiritual dimension, and was musically *healthy*, good for you, like raw carrots, in a way that Guns N' Roses wasn't.

It felt healthy because of the soothing (lullaby) effect of her voice. Healthy because it wasn't noisy or aggressive. Healthy because of the air, reverb, and space, like nature itself. Healthy because it was easy to listen to. And this meant that New Age could be added to the list of unchallenging, unthreatening, conservative genres that I already was trying to purge from my system. Enya was easy listening, therefore massively popular, and therefore vulgar.

Cool music isn't easy to listen to. It doesn't need to be liked on first listen. Gordon Gano from the Violent Femmes doesn't have a pleasing voice, so he doesn't need to be liked, he just needs to be heard. Sonic Youth's sound is noisy and dissonant, it's not trying to be pretty. It's anti-pretty. Aphex Twin makes us sit through multi-part structures that can't be understood until the twelfth listen. Bold and challenging rather than pandering to the masses. Heroic! Deep. Definitely not shallow.

Last night I was with some friends smoking weed and shooting the shit. A pianist friend and a grumpy painter were among the guests, and an argument arose about which record to play from an extensive jazz collection on vinyl. The pianist chose an album by the Modern Jazz Quartet which included Milt Jackson on vibraphone. The first chords sounded, then the vibraphone took over the melody. The painter scoffed at it and accused the pianist of preferring shallow music. Neither of these dudes were native English speakers, so there was some confusion about what the opposite of shallow music would be. We were trying to find the right word. "Deep" music?

The painter ran over to this collection and loudly touted that he had the right record: *Autumn Leaves*, Miles Davis.

The topic shifted to everyone's preferred desserts. Then there was a pause in the conversation as a trumpet solo started.

"This has depth. You feel it here," the painter said, touching his stomach.

"And the Modern Jazz Quartet is superficial?"

"It's easy listening! Cruise ship elevator music!"

The painter was probably referring to the sound of the vibraphone as elevator music. True enough, the vibraphone carried with it some untraceable connection to lounge music, to kitsch. Music that should be heard but not listened to closely. Background music.

So, this argument boils down to a faint sonic association of one particular instrument, the vibraphone. And even though Milt "Bags" Jackson was an undisputed vibraphone master, he couldn't escape something intrinsic in the instrument he had chosen as a teenager. Tough luck.

But my pianist friend wasn't convinced that the Miles Davis record was any deeper than the Modern Jazz Quartet.

I took a puff and said, "This is what my Enya book is about. This idea of music that sounds good while you eat or party or take a bath, versus music that you give your full attention to. And you guys are having the wrong argument. It's not that all music falls into these two categories. The goal of music should be to function on both levels. It's like with people."

The painter interrupted me. "You can't compare everything to everything."

I ignored him; he was always interrupting and making things more tense than they needed to be. "Some people you can shoot the shit with, make stupid jokes with, entertain each other. Some people you can have deeper conversations with, explore subjects that are uncomfortable, judgment-free intimacy. But the best people are the ones you can do both with."

I had talked about this subject in countless interviews: how I don't resent that my *Solo Piano* albums are often used as background music. My canned answer was something along the lines of "Hipster dinner parties require good background music, and I'm happy if I can fulfil that role."

When I moved to Berlin, I played piano in a Bavarian sausage restaurant, a hotel bar, and a posh ladies lingerie shop. Strictly atmosphere, no glory. But I was part of sacred activities: meals, clandestine meetings, the trying on of underwear. I respect the half-hidden nature of background music. I won't hate on it.

I just want my music to be useful. A French magazine once ran an exhaustive story on me and talked to French musicians I had collaborated with. Back then the biggest of these was Daft Punk. They asked Thomas Bangalter of Daft Punk about my music and he wrote that my piano album was the only thing that calmed down his newborn (human, not robot) child. One of my heroes had found that my album had a lullaby quality to it! My music served a function and it made me swell with pride.

The evening with the painter and the pianist ended with us rating iconic musicians. Rank from best to worst—Prince, the Beatles, Velvet Underground, David Bowie—that kind of thing. But before the painter could provide his ranking, he asked the existential question that Enya had forced me to ask: "Are we talking about quality and importance to the history of music, or just my taste?"

It's as if he felt a shadow hanging over him, the monolith of accepted taste hovering. He was aware of the canon, he could feel the heavy weight of history on his back, truths written on stone, but he also knew that his own actual preferences might diverge from these commandments. He was essentially asking permission to put his own twist on musical history. Even this misanthropic, unapologetic, opinionated artist was painfully self-aware of confessing an unpopular opinion. In a perfect world, he wouldn't need to qualify his choice of Prince over the Beatles (his pleasure, his opinion). But this world isn't perfect, so we all scurry around beneath the long-cast shadow of musical consensus.

As my research got more exhaustive, I happened upon a listicle of musicians who were asked to share their guilty pleasures. A lot of predictable answers, bubblegum pop, R&B, the usual suspects. Hit songs from hit artists that one wouldn't dare admit to respecting. Slash named Rihanna. Dave Grohl picked the Spice Girls. But Dev Hynes of Blood Orange, bless his heart, hit me straight in the gut with his answer: "Cyndi Lauper is a big, big idol of mine. She isn't a guilty pleasure, she is just as credible as the rest." Replace Cyndi with Enya, and I could've said it myself.

Back in my nineties Toronto days, when the indie-rock religion was strongest, and commercialism was simply not to be trusted in any circumstance, I had a friend who thought she'd found the solution to this consensus versus taste dilemma. It was an understandable and viable reaction: to laugh. Laughing in the face of music that lives in my writer friend's "importance to music history" and "my taste" chasm. It's always tempting to find a loophole, to ignore the premise of the problem, by discrediting both sides of the issue.

The argument went like this: Consensus thinking is for rule-followers and sheep who have no mind of their own. The guilty pleasure-seekers create a special category for music they like but know they shouldn't like. So how about listening enthusiastically to music that you identify as simply bad? It's kind of fun to mock the sincerity of music that has a direct, uncomplicated connection to its audience. In this worldview an Enya song isn't something to secretly enjoy, it is, by its very existence, proof of the stupidity of its listeners. It is garbage transformed by a marketing machine into fast food. And to listen to it while smirking at it is to resist the machine that created it.

These ironists can often be found in their natural habitat, the music scene of any urban centre. That's where I met my indie-rock zealot: the Rivoli on Queen Street West, alt-rock HQ circa 1997. She yelled into my ear drunkenly about how easy it would be to genetically engineer a shitty number-one hit. Hers was the cynic's lament: all you need is a big-name producer with a formula, a hook with a bunch of la la las or hey heys, a hot girl singer, and millions of dollars in record company support (there were actual record companies back then).

Fast forward to two hours later, the same girl was using her beer bottle as a microphone to lip-synch 4 Non Blondes "What's Up?": "Heeeeyyy, heeeeyy, heeeeey, what's going awwwn..."

I couldn't handle the hypocrisy so after the five minutes of this epic were finally over, I asked her if she even liked that song. She was louder and drunker and invading my personal space. I could smell beer when she screamed: "I fucking love it, it's so fucking bad!"

I've heard this argument dozens of times, how easy it would be to write hit songs. Well, if it's so easy, why don't you, etc.? I don't need to finish the obvious retort, do I? Well, on the other hand I do wish I could have written "What's Up?" or for that matter any of Enya's songs. The only difference is I know how difficult it is.

When I decided to write this, I tested out my idea on a few close friends. "I'm writing a book about Enya" seemed to provoke strong reactions. It reminded me of when I started to call myself "Chilly Gonzales, the musical genius." The raised eyebrows of disbelief, the nervous open-mouthed laughter, the strange grudging hiss of someone who needs to release some unwanted tension. That's when you know you're onto something. And of course, a few allies of mine instantly nodded and understood the power of invoking her. If they say they don't know Enya, they do. All I need to do is sing the words "sail away" three times to prod anyone's memory.

This was how I popped my Enya cherry, hearing "Sail Away" for the first time (it's actually called "Orinoco

Flow"). It was 1988, I was sixteen and obsessed with synthesizers. I may have discovered music through the piano, thanks to my grandfather, but the piano was his old-fashioned instrument, not mine. The synthesizer was my up-to-the-minute instrument, the sound of a modern teenager.

Enya used the JUNO-60, the DX7, but on "Orinoco Flow" it's the ROLAND D-50 that presides. This three hundred dollar keyboard with sixty keys creates an entire alternate sonic reality, an artificial recreation of real acoustic instruments—like a movie based on a true story. The D-50 has a sound called "trumpet," but it's not a real trumpet, it's just that the machine has identified the kinds of frequencies and waveforms that translate as trumpet-ish. Somehow our ear knows it's not a real trumpet but accepts the failed attempt.

But this failure has value—to me it has a poetic and dreamlike quality. "Trumpet" isn't trumpet but it captures an essence, much like a seemingly harmless caricature from an artist on Venice Beach can brutally reproduce a face with more truth than we'd like.

I eventually got my hands on a D-50. I would sit there scrolling through a list of exotic instrument names. Timpani! The Japanese koto! Bassoon! I had never seen or heard a bassoon, but as I played a few melodies on the D-50 copy of "bassoon" I was reminded of the jaunty circus intro of "Tears of a Clown" by Smokey Robinson. Then I played "bassoon" in a higher range up the keyboard... wait, isn't that the same sound as the pinched opening of Stravinsky's "The Rite of Spring"? This shitty copycat bassoon was real enough to shock me back to those musical memories like a Proustian Madeleine. I spent hours with headphones on, trying out every sound on the D-50, on a treasure hunt for the sound that launched "Orinoco Flow," until I found it: it was called "pizzicato strings."

When we think of bringing in the strings, we expect lush, sentimental, and expressive violins and cellos, the stuff of Hollywood movie endings. That's one way to tug on the heartstrings, and when we imagine a violinist, she is drawing a bow over the strings. In "Orinoco Flow," Enya's strings are played differently—pizzicato—the sound of a finger plucking the string.

Pizzicato is the less grandiose way of playing the violin. To me it sounds like a mandolin or even a banjo, so it transports me to a pre-classical, folk-music atmosphere. After all, the bow is an additional barrier between the human being and the string. Pizzicato cuts out the middleman, and we hear the tactile humanity of finger on string.

But remember, we're talking about a D-50 reproduction of pizzicato called "pizzicato strings." Enya sacrifices the tactile humanity of real augers in favour of the synthesized copy. Maybe the record company didn't want to pay a real string section for the debut album of a New Age artist. Maybe she just liked the sound of the D-50 better. Maybe her use of synthesized plucking was an aesthetic choice after the fact. One thing is sure about a synthesizer: it's predictable and consistent, as unchanging as a loyal friend. As a teenager, I sat there with my D-50 playing the "Sail Away" chords on patch 123, master of an entire orchestra, feeling both modern and ancient.

SAYING NO

DOWNBEAT MAGAZINE WAS THE BIBLE FOR JAZZ NERDS. I used to devour it the way other teenagers devoured porn magazines. My favourite section was the Blindfold Test. Some young up-and-coming musician would have to listen to random snatches of obscure jazz songs, and they would have to guess who was playing.

I tried to play my own blindfold test by listening to my local CBC jazz show. One afternoon the radio was on while I played Ping-Pong with my best friend, and a song came on that I'd never heard. It sounded like something from the sixties, but I wasn't sure—other than I liked it. But after just two short trumpet blasts, I suddenly knew I was hearing Miles Davis. My unconscious had identified him as I would have the speaking voice of my best friend—and indeed my friend was very impressed that I'd won my blindfold test. I felt like I had a superpower (even though it was Miles who was the superhero).

Now if I hear a half-bar of fake synthesized string plucking, I know it's Enya. That's what we call a signature sound. And not everyone is Miles Davis or Enya. It's usually the singing voice that burrows deep inside your unconscious, making it instantly identifiable. A voice is like a face in sonic form. You can't describe it in words, but you create a little file in your mental hard drive: that's David Bowie's voice, that's my sister's, that's Barack Obama's, that annoying one is Björk's. It reminds me of the marketing campaign for Celine Dion (when she released her first English-language album) that claimed: "Remember the name because you will never forget the voice."

A signature sound is reassuring when you recognize it, like a familiar routine. I go to Café Hommage every day and order the same galette with goat's cheese and honey, a flat white with oat milk and a fresh apple juice with ginger—a true hipster's feast. I know what to expect and I feel control over my own happiness. I don't want any surprises. Why would I want an uninvited banana on my plate? You know I hate them!

I was shocked as a child when my mother came home with a perm and I thought, *who is this curly-haired impostor?* I have the same impulse when I put on a brand-new Lana Del Rey album. I'm comforted by the orchestral intros and the lazy melancholy of her voice. I wouldn't want her to suddenly start screaming in falsetto over distorted banjos.

A signature sound is made of ingredients that we get used to, but we can't overlook the missing ingredients, the things that aren't there. The things we *don't* like.

It's hard for me to trust a musician who says they like every ingredient. You know the type: "I like everything from Abba to Zappa." I've worked with some session musicians (with or without ponytails) who go from gig to gig, from studio date to studio date. They might be called upon to play reggae on Monday, heavy metal on Tuesday. They can *play* it all, so they start to believe that they *love* it all. They would rather play tastefully than to have taste. But to me, art suffers if the artist likes everything.

It's a question I ask classical musicians when I meet them: "Who do you hate?" Classical music education is a massive ass-kiss to the usual suspects, the canon of accepted genius composers. The conservatory got its name from being quite literally conservative, and the consensus handed down is not to be questioned. It's as dogmatic as the Catholic Church but with more syphilis. So, the classical musician has to have mighty big balls to reject one of these Great Men of the Pantheon. I asked the question to Igor Levit, a pianist who's recorded obscure and notoriously unplayable works, and without blinking an eye he sneered, "Chopin." Now here was a musician I could get along with.

I became obsessed with this theory, that what an artist doesn't like is more important than what they like. Perhaps we had gotten the whole taste equation wrong, maybe it wasn't our favourite band that mattered but the one we hated. Maybe I should have written this book about my contempt for loud singers. (Maybe I did!)

I explored this further when I held my inaugural Gonzervatory (a music performance workshop) in 2018. I designed the written application to include "name an artist who musicians all seem to love that you hate." The answers were all over the place. Some pop-haters who hadn't really understood the question mentioned Justin Bieber or Taylor Swift—typical guilty pleasures.

Some applicants refused to play along, proclaiming some resistance to putting negative energy out into the world. They were the "I like everything" types. Wrong answer. Then there were the easy targets: Radiohead, Coldplay, bands who seem to take themselves very seriously. I could get with that, but it didn't seem radical enough.

Then I read the application of a South American singer-songwriter who simply wrote "Prince." It actually shocked me, as I revered Prince the way classical musicians revered Mozart. I realized just how powerful this question could be, and that candidate made it to the shortlist of applicants just for having the balls to go against a god among (most) musicians.

A choice against something has power; it has resistance. This power goes supernova when the choice is against something that everyone expects or craves.

I can't count the number of times I've been asked why I don't combine electronic elements with my piano onstage. For some reason, many fans would think it obvious for me to have a laptop sitting on top of the piano where the sheet music normally goes, a glowing white Apple shining unmysteriously on a darkened concert hall stage.

But to me that's corny, I would do anything for (an audience's) love, but I won't do that.

And my music sounds different thanks to this rejection. I've forced myself to find ways to make the music *feel* mechanical, modern, and electronic without the easy crutch of actually using electronics. This choice I made is a frame that excludes using electronics onstage. It's a precondition, a manifesto, a border I won't cross. It's the constitution of my musical country, against which all future laws will be measured.

The poet Ted Hughes writes about using limits in poetry-writing exercises in his book *Poetry in the Making*: "Artificial limits create a crisis, which rouses the brain's resources, the compulsion towards haste overthrows the ordinary precautions, flings everything into top gear, and many things that are hidden find themselves rushed into the open. Barriers break down, prisoners come out of their cells." This is the contradiction at the heart of creativity: constraints set us free.

This book exists because of constraints. There is no more terrifying moment than when staring at the blank page. The German publisher of this book has been asking me to write a musical memoir for years, but I was the victim of that empty space in which anything and everything can happen. And in this infinity of possibilities, existential doubt creeps in. If I can do *anything* right now, I'll never be sure of my choice. I'll be like a session musician with no actual taste. I told the publisher of my failure and moved on to other projects.

A couple of years later I met my friend Sophie Passmann at Café Hommage for my usual goat's cheese galette. She had written a book about Frank Ocean for this same publisher, as part of a series called MusikBibliothek. Each author would write about a single artist—and despite there being two female authors, all four books in the series were about dudes.

"If I was going to write one of these I'd have to write about a woman. How many pages is it again?" I asked.

"My Frank Ocean book is around eighty pages."

"So, I should write eighty pages about…" and here I have to admit I surprised myself by what I blurted out: "Enya."

It was almost a joke that rose up from my unconscious. But it was my way in. With Enya as a constraint, I could finally write a musical memoir, the very book the publisher had asked for years ago. And I got there first by deciding what *not* to write about: another dude.

So here we are, a book about Enya that analyzes her voice, her chord progressions and her synthesizer sounds: the elements of her signature sound. But what ingredients does she leave out? I will imagine now asking her the question I asked of the French session musicians, Igor Levit, and my Gonzervatory applicants: "Enya, what do you hate?"

Drums, for starters. No drum set, no fills, no beats. Drum-lessness.

These days when a car passes by at two in the morning, all I hear is drums: low 808 kick-drum pollution expelled by a subwoofer. Or when I'm sitting in a taxi and the radio is on the lowest possible volume setting, I only hear the sounds of stuttering hi-hats and sibilant shakers (who listens to the radio at that volume anyway?).

As a pianist, it's hard to imagine drums as the most important part of music. When I first moved to Berlin I started collaborating with an electronic producer. The most awkward sessions began with the producer searching mindlessly through a digital folder of drum sounds, with names like hellkik22.wav or slithersnap. aiff. This process could eat up precious minutes of what could otherwise be music-making. It felt like we were spending way too much time choosing paint-brushes instead of, you know, starting to paint.

Luckily, I found my way to hanging out with pro-ducers like Peaches or Tiga—songwriters who just so happened to use electronic drums. It turns out some of them are even Enya fans. A DJ friend of mine, Teki Latex, sometimes begins his sets with "Orinoco Flow," although he told me, "I add a beat." This is, after all, dance music, and getting people to dance is a DJ's prime directive. Dance music without drums is comedy without laughter. But Enya isn't trying to get you to dance, so she doesn't need the beat.

Her approach to drums comes from a much older era: the orchestral percussion section. In the or-chestra drums don't really do very much. The great cliché about orchestral drummers is that they have to wait forty minutes to hit the giant bass drum once (and that they're all alcoholics as a result).

They are cursed to be used as an occasional detail. The percussionists rarely play any "grooves" in classical music, other than the occasional military march banged out on a solitary snare.

Enya's solution is to reject beats altogether and instead focus on the single grand gestures of symphonic percussion: majestic timpani and whooshing cymbals. Subtle gestures that the ear hardly notices. Enya with a fat beat would just sound wrong. (Maybe the exception is the Fugees who actually tried it with "Ready or Not," sampling her song "Boadicea").

Rejecting beats may be a radical act in our time. It may just be that Enya has the beat playing in her head already, and simply chooses to leave it out. Thanks to those borderline-harsh pizzicato stabs, Enya attains rhythmic drive by other means. My friend Teki Latex may have added a beat when he DJs this song, but this just isn't necessary to get my head nodding. Paradoxically, for me, drum-lessness creates energy. It's a magic trick that makes the song stand out as an unlikely earworm.

The orchestral fetish is strong in Enya, to the point where her own voice is often pushed aside. It turns out that the pipes that soothed and sold millions are often absent. On *The Very Best of Enya* compilation, half of the songs feature her as a lead singer, another twenty-five percent treats her voice as an orchestral instrument (no words), while the last twenty-five percent is strictly instrumental. Her secret weapon, her money-maker, lying unused. In its place, a wordless space for the instruments to tell a story.

There is a dividing line between songs and instrumental music. If we squint at the first few centuries of classical music, the Italians invented opera. In opera, voice is king, with the orchestra of a lower rank, quite literally submerged in a pit invisible to the audience. The Germans countered with wordless absolute music—the sonata and the symphony. In absolute music, this sidekick orchestra rises to the status of hero. The plot and intrigue of operatic storytelling are transmuted into the abstract and subjective.

Enya is no operatic figure—that lullaby voice would never have cut through in an opera house. No, what I hear in her long vocal silences is a belief in the power of absolute music, a way of telegraphing her completeness as an artist, not *just* a singer. It's another counterintuitive Enya move.

Remembering how often fans and journalists alike would assume that Peaches (a genius producer) didn't make her own beats, I can hardly imagine the frustration of being constantly underestimated as a musician by being a singing female. But pressing play on Enya's second album, I remember hearing "Watermark" (a spare piano instrumental) followed by "Cursum Perficio" (multiple backing Enyas chanting in Latin), and finally "On Your Shore," in which her voice takes centre stage. This slow-motion rollout of the singer Enya told me I was dealing with a visionary composer who also happened to have a voice for the ages.

Wordlessness works for me. I was never a lyrics junkie outside of my affection for listening to rap. Rap lyrics are direct, playful, and journalistic, standing in contrast to the impressionistic, poetic style of singer songwriters. With some exceptions (Leonard Cohen is the only one I can think of right now) I listen to music where the lyrics are in the passenger seat. No one really hears or cares what the Bee Gees are singing about, and I doubt that a single Bee Gee would even dispute that. Prince had some memorable one-liners—"act your age, not your shoe size"—but the words are secondary. Cohen said he would spend an eternity finishing a twelve-line poem before even picking up a guitar. On the other hand, it sounds like Prince shoehorns his phrases into the groove at the last minute. Dissecting disembodied Bee Gees lyrics on a page will likely leave any reader underwhelmed. But most people of taste own a book of Leonard Cohen verse.

The voice carries the emotion, not necessarily the words. My favourite band Beach House gets me in my feelings, and yet I misunderstand most of their lyrics, buried as they are under a haze of organ and woozy guitars. I don't need to know the words, because the song is already crying (as Jay-Z implies). From a technical perspective, this effect is created by mixing the vocals at a lower-than-expected volume (after drums, vocals are usually the loudest element in pop music).

When she does sing lyrics, Enya isn't the author who writes them (they are based on poems by long-time collaborator Roma Ryan). This kind of lifelong composer/lyricist mind-meld divides up the jobs neatly. Schubert famously set the words of Goethe to music, and Mozart had his librettos written by Lorenzo Da Ponte. So, Enya strikes me as more of a nineteenth century Romantic composer than a modern-day singer-songwriter.

On "Orinoco Flow," the words are embedded within the music and shadowed in reverb. A French friend of mine thought that it was a Christmas song, because instead of "sail away" he heard "c'est Noel"—it's Christmas. (Enya eventually released a Christmas-themed album, so there might be something to this misunderstanding.)

Enya has also sung many songs in an invented language known as Loxian (sample: "Syoombraya").

The hierarchy of music over lyrics isn't even in question anymore. And when she wrote three songs for *The Lord of the Rings* films, she obviously chose to sing in Quenya, an Elvish language (I found it strange that the name Enya is hidden in that word). To our ears these invented languages are musicalized nonsense, but nonetheless they can supply an indirect emotional kick.

In fact, the French have a name for this principle: *yaourt* (French for yogurt). This language system does not consist of actual words, but of word-like syllables that are created by spontaneous mouth-shapes. Many singer-songwriters have brought me demos that include lyrics consisting only of *yaourt* and it requires imagination and discipline to not simply hear gibberish.

The writing of a melody is so delicate. But finding the perfect words takes time. So *yaourt* is the temporary fix that allows composition to continue. Music first! And at some later date, these *yaourt* syllables will find their real-language equivalents. In using an invented language, Enya rejects the overreliance on words—it's as if her songs stay in a state of "yogurt."

Researching this book, I understood that her entire career could be characterized as wordless. There are only a dozen deep-dive Enya interviews in existence. But any decent promotion campaign has to be omnipresent, overwhelming and on-message. They'll insist that it must "tell a story." This, of course, would mandate the artist's full commitment to a gruelling, punishing media schedule. It demands physical and mental effort far surpassing what it took to birth the album—the opposite of fun.

My musician friends and I constantly scheme on how to do less of it without sabotaging our work. What kind of balls would it take to just say no to this torture? Enya's balls, that's what. Her songs teach the lesson of letting the music speak for itself. And so, it is in her public persona, a voice that is reluctant and scarce, and the more powerful for it.

Some friends suggested I try to interview Enya for this book. To what end? Not only would she reject me, if I did manage to get fifteen minutes with her, it might kill some of the (chaste) fantasies I have about her. No, I need to respect the wordlessness.

And as these rejections of convention begin to accumulate, an image comes to mind: the exploding heads of record executives. "An instrumental to start off the new album? No weeklong media blitz in Portugal? At least she'll head out on a concert tour, right?"

It turns out that Enya has rejected this too.

When bands get older and more comfortable, the touring lifestyle loses its lustre. The golden years tend to be those first trips in a van out of town, sleeping on audience members' couches, a tribe moving under cover of darkness from town to town. The second phase involves swanky hotels but the cracks in the facade start to show. Then the drummer has a kid and it's the beginning of the end of the road. The schedule slows to a trickle.

Enya skipped directly to the end and has never gone on tour. Another rejection, her balls on full display. When we romanticize the uncompromising artist, who courageously accepts the consequences of rule-breaking, we could be tempted to think of a confrontational Kanye or an unpredictable Grimes. But let's remember that Enya has been playing by her own rules, right under our noses, since 1998.

She even said no to the closing credits song for the highest-grossing movie of all time, a rejection of *Titanic* proportions. She said no to giving a talk to Harvard Business School about her business strategy of saying no. And just imagine the nos that we're not aware of! Nos upon nos, how many? Who knows?

If I had sold millions of copies of my first album, I might have uncovered that same Enya courage. It was easy for her to be a badass, because she had that fuck-you leverage. The record company douches had no choice but to release her music on her terms. As for me, I didn't have that leverage. So, I said yes to everything, to anything that could move the ball forward even a millimetre. The voice in my head rationalized: "My desperation is necessary, I simply don't have a choice!" But that was just a convenient story I told myself. Behind this fairy tale was a tragic reality. My ego had the loudest voice in the room when I made decisions. There wasn't any oxygen left for my true artist voice, it just couldn't compete.

My philosophy was a desperate version of Gore Vidal's famous advice to "never miss a chance to have sex or appear on television." When *Solo Piano* came out, I fantasized about the exponential power of a certain French TV talk show. If I could just get onto that screen and into people's homes to play my single "Gogol," surely my album would blow up. I found out that the odds were stacked against me as a non-singing instrumentalist.

You see, a TV producer's greatest existential fear is that a viewer will change the channel during an instrumental piece. In this brutal TV-mindset, a boring singer is better than an exciting pianist. So, they started proposing all manner of compromises: a funny cover of an eighties song (remember when I wrote about how easy and powerful a gimmick this is?). Or leading the audience in a singalong, or better yet, giving the tanned, coked-up TV host a piano lesson. I wish I had said no. I wish I had stood up for myself and walked out in a huff, as if to say, "not without my daughter."

But instead I simply said, "Thank you, when and where should I show up?"

I went through the motions of "teaching" the TV host something or other about scales, and after we negotiated real hard, I was grudgingly permitted to pivot to playing forty-five seconds of "Gogol." I was vindicated, sort of. TV is all-powerful. For the following two weeks I was recognized all over Paris in a way I wasn't used to. My face had been on that communal screen, it had travelled further than my music ever had. The barista at my café had seen it. A random guy on a bus shouted "pianiste" at me. I walked into the dermatologist's office and the receptionist studied my face for a few seconds. Then I saw her hands and fingers gesticulating as if to say, "You're a guy I saw play piano." She certainly didn't know my beloved "Gogol," she just knew she'd seen me, and everyone around me told me it went well, mission accomplished (in a George W. Bush kind of way). But going to bed that night I knew I had displeased the gods of music.

It took me fifteen years to learn to say no. It was excruciating at first, like building a muscle that didn't previously exist. It soon became a reflex, a habit, muscle memory. Now my tongue coils behind my teeth, lying in wait, as I hear someone's undignified proposition. "We want you to compose music for a tuba choir to accompany our exhibition of digitally animated vintage photographs."

I just can't wait to say it.

NO!

But back then, it was a reflexive knee-jerk YES! How could I have thrown "Gogol" under a bus like that? Didn't my work deserve more protection, more security, more… love?

Artists often talk in interviews about their works as "babies." How can they choose a favourite song that they've written, that's like picking a favourite child! You especially hear these kinds of analogies from childless artists.

It reminds me of another artist interview trope: "My songs/books/paintings are my therapy." For me, being creative was a positive step toward releasing forbidden feelings. As my friend Jarvis Cocker said, "The artist learns about himself by making stuff." My shrink would call it sublimation, and it's better than nothing. Making music likely kept me from far less healthy pursuits. (Hitler was a frustrated artist after all.)

During my own lengthy psychotherapy, a recurring theme emerged: that I needed to be my own "good mother." It seems simple, right? Whatever lack, whatever hole, whatever void exists within can be filled with positive, compensating energy. Be your own sunshine, love yourself, all of that bullshit.

But as I wrote in my song "Self-Portrait":

> This self-portrait, I wanna torch it
> I love it but I wanna divorce it
> Who's there? It's only despair,
> I try to avoid the void, but it's just there

Not only does it rhyme, but it captures my frustration at achieving self-awareness without the ability to—you know—actually change. It's a kind of paralysis, knowing that the void isn't empty at all. In fact, the void needs to be emptied before it can be filled. It stinks and it's overflowing with psychic trash, and... there is a garbage strike? (This metaphor is being stretched too far.)

So, first the void needs to be emptied and writing a rap seems to be the only tool available to me to make this happen. When I write verses like in "Self-Portrait," it is emptied out just a little. Sublimation wins again, creativity as safety valve, four rhyming lines sending the bad mother into exile.

But now I'm exhausted and can't find the energy

to fill that void with something better. Inside the void there is just paralysis. I need help from the outside. I need the right atmosphere to regroup. I need better lighting to heal myself. I need the right soundtrack.

This outside help is the true description of my musical taste—my *true* musical taste, the one that gives me involuntary goosebumps, not the received taste of journalists' top ten lists. The songs I turn to in trying times are the background music of filling the void, the original score to the movie of my life. My own mother didn't soothe me with lullabies, but in music I could find that warm maternal energy. If I can't quite be my own good mother, I'll find one in music.

I found one in music, and her name is Enya.

So wait, the trope is true after all? Songs are therapy?

Well, no. Therapy is therapy. And children are children. Sure, there are superficial similarities between the creation of artworks and the creation of children. My songs are shepherded into existence, they contain traces of me, their creator. I feel an instinctive connection to my *Solo Piano* album, I could probably cuddle with it, I'm even convinced my life would have been worse off without it. In moments of extreme self-regard I even think it will outlast me.

I am responsible for *Solo Piano* as it moves through the world. Back in the era of saying yes to everything,

I came up short. Like dealing with a child, I should have set more boundaries. I should have been more like good mother Enya, who holds her songs close and doesn't let go.

Yes, *Solo Piano* needed my protection, and I learned the hard way. Good old "Gogol" was used in an online bank commercial in France back in 2008, and for some reason it has stayed on the air every year since, prominently featured in ad breaks during France's most popular talk show. Yes, *that* talk show.

To this day, I can't perform the piece in France without hearing dozens of sibilant audience whispers, undoubtedly trying to place where they know the piece from. It's especially frustrating given that it's the first piece of the entire *Solo Piano* trilogy, and it works perfectly as the opener in any concert. Just not in Lyon or Bordeaux. Or Paris. The only loophole I found is to make a routine out of it, but the laughter is hollow. The truth is that in one country, the piece doesn't belong to me anymore—it is a child I gave away for adoption, whose new parents are an Internet finance corporation. Cha-ching, but boo-hoo.

Enya put her own twist on this, casting music as a stand-in for a love interest. In a rare interview, she was asked why she never started a family. She answered, "My affairs are with melody and words and beautiful sounds." True, she doesn't have children, and is by her own admission anti-social, private, and uninterested in personal fame. This book will respect that privacy. If songs are her therapy, or her children, or her lovers, we don't need to speculate further. They are precious to her, and to us.

EPILOGUE

NO RULE IS WITHOUT ITS EXCEPTION. I've always loved Enya's music, but I didn't know much about her when I decided to write this book. I just followed a hunch. The more I read about her, and the more I saw my friends' reaction to her name, the more I could feel myself slipping into a fantasy: Enya the good mother, the unguilty pleasure, the uber-artist. But no good mother is one hundred percent good, and no bad mother is one hundred percent bad. It's too easy to say that she is beyond reproach when I want so badly for it to be true.

And as I got close to the end of my first draft, I was steered toward a YouTube video that brutally popped the bubble of this fantasy. It's a television commercial for Volvo from 2013. The first image is of Belgian muscleman/actor Jean-Claude Van Damme, eyes closed in deep concentration. We hear the opening synthesized plucks of Enya's "Only Time" begin to play. The camera pans out to reveal two Volvo trucks driving along the highway, and Van Damme is revealed to be standing with one leg on each of the truck's side mirrors. The trucks slowly separate. The surreal climax of this commercial is Van Damme doing the splits between these speeding vehicles, soundtracked by that lullaby voice that has soothed me countless times.

I had so many questions. Was this a homemade goof video made by some Internet prankster? No, it was a real, official Volvo TV advertisement. A pitch had been approved, contracts had been signed, money had exchanged hands.

Suddenly I remembered that Enya lives in a castle and has sold eighty million albums. No artist is above the rules of commerce, even Enya. There are moments when we simply can't say no, and even my good mother has her price.

ABOUT THE AUTHOR

Chilly Gonzales, Grammy-winning Canadian pianist and entertainer currently living in Europe, is known as much for the intimate piano touch of his best-selling *Solo Piano* album trilogy as for his showmanship and composition for award-winning stars.

Gonzo aims to be a man of his time, approaching the piano with classical and jazz training but with the attitude of a rapper. He performs and writes songs with Jarvis Cocker, Feist, and Drake, among others and holds the Guinness world record for the longest solo concert at over twenty-seven hours. In 2014 he won a Grammy for his collaboration on Daft Punk's Best Album of the Year. 2018 saw the cinema release of a career retrospective documentary *Shut Up and Play the Piano* that premiered at the A-list Berlinale Film festival.

Gonzales is also a respected writer, broadcaster, and "musical scientist," as seen in his hit web series Pop Music Masterclass, BBC Radio 1 documentary Classical Connections, The History of Music on Arte and Apple Music's Beats1 radio show Music's Cool with Chilly Gonzales. Most recently, Chilly Gonzales ventured into a new form of entrepreneurship. A culmination of recent years' explorations in teaching, Gonzo inaugurated his very own music school: The Gonzervatory.

THE BIBLIOPHONIC SERIES is a catalogue of the ongoing history of contemporary music. Each book is a time capsule, capturing artists and their work as we see them, providing a unique look at some of today's most exciting musicians.

INVISIBLE PUBLISHING produces fine Canadian literature for those who enjoy such things. As a not-for-profit publisher, our work includes building communities that sustain and encourage engaging, literary, and current writing.

Invisible Publishing has been in operation for over a decade. We released our first fiction titles in the spring of 2007, and our catalogue has come to include works of graphic fiction and non-fiction, pop culture biographies, experimental poetry, and prose.

We are committed to publishing diverse voices and experiences. In acknowledging historical and systemic barriers, and the limits of our existing catalogue, we strongly encourage writers from LGBTQ2SIA+ communities, Indigenous writers, and writers of colour to submit their work.

Invisible Publishing is also home to the Bibliophonic series of music books and the Throwback series of CanLit reissues.

If you'd like to know more, please get in touch:
info@invisiblepublishing.com